Chapter 1: A Divided Country

In the mid-1800s, there were many differences between the Northern and Southern United States. In both areas, most people were farmers. However, in the North, there were also many factories. Workers were paid to make products such as farm machinery and cloth, which were sold around the country.

In the South, there were very few factories. Most people owned or worked on farms. Crops like cotton, tobacco, and rice were grown on huge **plantations**. A plantation needed hundreds of workers. Most of these workers were slaves who belonged to the plantation owners.

This slave family is picking cotton in Georgia.

TIME LINE

March 1820	September 1850	November 1860	December 1860	February 1861
Missouri Compromise.	Compromise of 1850.	Abraham Lincoln elected president.	South Carolina secedes.	Confederate States of America established.

Arguments about slavery

Slavery had existed in the United States since **colonial** days. There had always been people who thought slavery was wrong. As the country grew, so did the arguments over slavery.

By the mid-1800s, many settlers were moving into **territories** in the west. People disagreed about whether slavery should be allowed in the new territories. Then, the territories began to become states. Some Americans thought each state should be able to decide whether to become a slave state or a free state. Others thought the U.S. government should make those decisions.

Conditions in northern factories were not always as nice and clean as the factory pictured here.

September 1862	July 1863	November 1864	April 1865	April 1861
Emancipation Proclamation.	Battle of Gettysburg.	Lincoln reelected.	Confederate army surrenders; Lincoln is killed.	First battle of the Civil War at Fort Sumter.

In 1820 the Missouri Compromise allowed slavery in Missouri. However, it made slavery illegal in the North. The Compromise of 1850 also said that the **territory** of California would join the Union as a free state.

In 1860 Abraham Lincoln became president of the United States. He had promised to keep slavery out of the territories. Many Southerners were upset when he was elected. Soon afterward, South Carolina announced that it was **seceding** from the Union, which meant that it was leaving the United States. Within a few months, ten other states did the same. These states formed a new government that allowed slavery. The new government was called the Confederate States of America, or the Confederacy.

Lincoln said the United States could not survive if states could secede whenever they wanted. He was willing to go to war to keep the Union together.

This map shows the United States at the start of the Civil War.

The war begins

The North was better prepared for war than the South. The Union army had more soldiers and money. There were many factories in the North in which weapons could be made.

Both sides thought that they would win the war quickly.

In July 1861, the Union and Confederate armies fought their first big battle in Manassas Junction, Virginia, by a small stream called Bull Run. The Confederacy referred to the battle as "The Battle of Bull Run." Its official name is "The Battle of Manassas."

Many people thought it would be interesting to watch the fighting. They came with picnic baskets to sit and watch. They had no idea how terrible the day would be.

Lincoln in his last formal photograph, taken on the day the Confederacy surrendered.

Neither army was ready for battle. Many of the leaders had never fought in an actual war. Most of the soldiers were volunteers with little or no training. The leaders weren't sure what orders to give. The soldiers weren't good at following orders. As a result, neither the leaders nor the soldiers knew what to do.

The fighting went on all day. Toward the end of the battle, fresh Confederate troops arrived. The Union troops gave up and returned to Washington, D.C. The South won the battle, but many soldiers died on both sides. Everyone could now see that the war was going to be a long one.

The Emancipation Proclamation

Maryland, Kentucky, Missouri, and Delaware were known as border states. These states were located in between the South and the North. They allowed slavery but had not **seceded** from the Union. Both sides wanted the states to join them. One of the reasons the states were considered valuable was that they had factories in which weapons could be made.

Lincoln was under pressure from **abolitionists** to end slavery. Lincoln himself hated slavery, but his greatest concern was to restore the Union. He wanted to find a way to end slavery without losing the border states. In 1862 Lincoln signed the Emancipation Proclamation. This document freed the slaves in the Confederate states. It did not free slaves in the border states.

"Uncle Tom's Cabin" by Harriet Beecher Stowe helped inform people in the north about slavery.

135,000 SETS, 270,000 VOLUMES SOLD.

UNCLE TOM'S CABIN

FOR SALE HERE

AN EDITION FOR THE MILLION, COMPLETE IN 1 Vol., PRICE 37 1-2 CENTS.
"   "   IN GERMAN, IN 1 Vol., PRICE 50 CENTS.
"   "   IN 2 Vols,. CLOTH, 6 PLATES, PRICE $1.50.
SUPERB ILLUSTRATED EDITION, IN 1 Vol., WITH 153 ENGRAVINGS,
PRICES FROM $2.50 TO $5.00.

The Greatest Book of the Age

The end of the war

Union troops marched toward Vicksburg, Mississippi, in April 1863. They laid **siege** to the city for about a month and

a half. That meant no one could enter or leave. With no new supplies, the people inside the city began to starve. On July 4, 1863, the Confederate army gave up and turned Vicksburg over to the Union army. On the same date, a three-day battle ended in Gettysburg, Pennsylvania. Many men died in the battle. For the North, it was a turning point. After the battle at Gettysburg, the Union started to win most battles.

The war continued for almost two more years. The fighting destroyed much of the South. Farms, towns, and entire cities such as Atlanta, Georgia, were in ruins.

On April 9, 1865, the Confederate army gave up. Its leader, General Robert E. Lee, met Union General Ulysses S. Grant at Appomattox Courthouse, Virginia. Lee officially surrendered, ending the Civil War.

After the war, a long period known as Reconstruction began in the South. The goal of Reconstruction was to rebuild the South and to help the freed slaves begin their new lives.

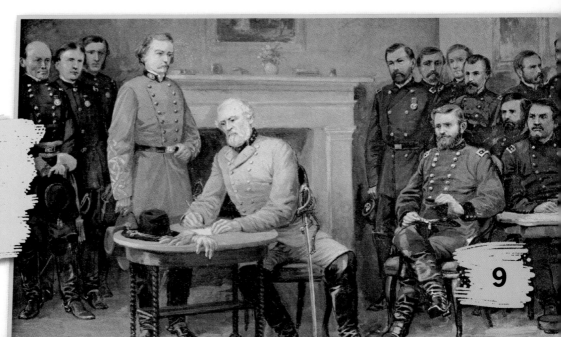

General Lee surrenders to General Grant at Appomattox Court House.

Chapter 2: Life During the War

The Civil War affected all Americans. Thousands of young men volunteered as soldiers. Thousands more were drafted, or required, to serve in the army. Some schools closed because so many teachers and students went off to war. Women and children were left to take care of farms and businesses.

The war was especially hard on Southerners. Most of the fighting took place in the South. During battles, large areas of cities such as Richmond, Virginia, burned to the ground. Soldiers from both armies destroyed crops to keep food from the enemy. Also, many slaves who worked on **plantations** escaped to the North. Even if crops weren't destroyed, there might not be anyone left to plant and harvest them. By the end of the war, food was in short

When Union forces entered Richmond, Virginia on April 3, 1865, they found much of the city destroyed by fire.

supply in many parts of the South. Slaves suffered from the shortages even more than other people. This was because they were usually the last people to be given food.

Other items were in short supply as well. The South had depended on goods from Northern factories and supplies imported from other countries. During the war, the Union navy **blockaded** Southern ports. Supply ships couldn't reach the South. There wasn't enough flour, coffee, leather, or cotton. People couldn't get enough coal for heat or lamp oil for light.

This woman is being fitted for a hoop skirt, a lengthy process.

WARTIME DRESSES

In the 1860s, wide hoop skirts were in fashion. However, during the war, Southern woman couldn't get enough cloth to make hoop skirts. So they started to make dresses with smaller skirts.

A slave's life

Life as a slave in the South was difficult. Slaves were not allowed to decide where or when to work. They were not allowed to own property. Family members were often split up by being sold to different owners. Slaves could be punished severely for minor crimes, or for no reason at all.

The kind of **plantation** a slave worked on and the kind of work he or she did determined the kind of life the slave led. Slaves on cotton plantations worked for hours in the hot sun. They picked cotton all day, work that was hard on their hands and backs. Life on a tobacco plantation was similar. Slaves cleared fields for growing new tobacco. When the fields were cleared, the slaves planted the tobacco. Then they picked it when it was ready.

Life on rice plantations was usually a little easier. Each slave was assigned a task, or project to complete. When the task was finished, the slave was done working for the day.

A white land owner oversees cotton picking in Texas.

Some slaves worked inside their owners' homes. These slaves worked as housekeepers, butlers, nannies, cooks, carriage drivers, and carpenters. Sometimes they thought of themselves as part of their owner's family. Sometimes these slaves did not want to leave their owners, even after being freed.

Ways to freedom

Slaves often ran away. Some slaves used The Underground Railroad. The "railroad" was a system of houses and people who helped slaves escape. Most of the people working on the Underground Railroad were black **abolitionists**. Many of them were former slaves themselves.

Most slaves could not read and did not have maps. On many plantations, slaves were not allowed to meet in large groups or meet with slaves from other plantations. Slaves still found ways to communicate. Sometimes seemingly harmless songs or rhymes held secret messages. Another more complicated way of passing messages was through quilts. Slaves often sewed secret messages into the patterns of quilts.

This small house in New York City was once part of the Underground Railroad.

Chapter 3: Rest and Relaxation

Life in the army

Finding and eating food was an important part of daily life for soldiers in both armies. Union soldiers were often fighting far away from home in areas where people were unhappy to see them. Food had to be brought in from the North. One frequent meal was hardtack, a type of cracker baked in the North.

Soldiers on both sides often played instruments and sang songs around the camp before and after dinner. Popular songs of the Union Army included "The Battle Hymn of the Republic" and "When Johnny Comes Marching Home." Popular songs of the Confederate Army included "Yellow Rose of Texas" and "Dixie." Some army regiments even had their own bands.

These union officers are being waited on during their meal.

Singing was also popular on both home fronts. Two popular songs were "Oh Susanna" and "Camptown Races."

Soldiers who could write sent letters home. Some of those letters still exist today. Those who could not write often had someone else write out what they wanted to say. Soldiers were eager for any reading material they could find.

Even during the war, people found time for fun. Baseball was already an old game by the time of the Civil War. Soldiers played versions of it around camp. They also used cannon balls as makeshift bowling balls.

THE BATTLE HYMN OF THE REPUBLIC

Poet Julia Ward Howe wrote the popular Union song "The Battle Hymn of the Republic". The song was based on a popular song about the abolitionist John Brown. Howe sold the song to *The Atlantic Monthly* magazine for five dollars in 1862.

Soldiers often had long, empty periods of time on their hands.

Women during the war

Women often found themselves with new responsibilities after the war began. Some women chose to participate in the war itself. Dr. Mary Walker served as a surgeon's assistant for the Union. She was taken prisoner by the Confederate Army. Dr. Walker is the only woman to have ever received the U.S. Medal of Honor. Women on both sides served as spies and nurses for the army. Some women also dressed up as men and joined the army. Sarah Edmonds did all three. Edmonds dressed as a man and joined the Union Army. While in the army she sometimes "pretended" to be a woman so that she could spy on nearby Confederate troops. She later served as an army nurse.

Clara Barton was the founder of the Red Cross.

ANGELS OF THE BATTLEFIELD

Two of the most famous Civil War nurses, known as Angels of the Battlefield, were Clara Barton and Dorothea Dix. Many people were reluctant to send female nurses to the front lines. Both these women proved that female nurses were needed and as capable as men. Clara Barton went on to become the founder of the American Red Cross. Many men also served as nurses during the Civil War, including the poet Walt Whitman.

The life of a child

Boys as young as ten or twelve served as drummers and flute players in the army. They often led their regiments directly into war. While their fathers were at war, children at home often had new responsibilities and chores. Most children still found time to play, however. Children during the Civil War played with many of the same toys and games as children today. They went swimming and climbed trees. They played baseball, hide-and-seek, marbles, and checkers. Their toys included dolls, slingshots, and toy guns.

Johnny Clem, a drummer boy, was only twelve when this photo was taken. He became a hero after the Battle of Shiloh.

By doing the hands-on activities and crafts in this chapter, you'll get a sense of what life was like for people who lived during the Civil War.

Recipe: Bake Hardtack

Union soldiers received a daily ration, or single serving, of hardtack. When it was fresh, hardtack was easy to eat. However, most hardtack was months old before it got to soldiers. By then, it was so hard, some soldiers broke a tooth eating it. You should eat your hardtack right away while it is fresh. If it gets hard, dunk it in milk before eating.

WARNING !

Always make sure an adult is present when using a hot stove.

Make sure to read all the directions before starting the recipe.

These Union soldiers are in Hilton Head, South Carolina. Today the area is a posh resort, with better food.

1. Preheat the oven to 400°F.

2. Grease the cookie sheet with butter, margarine, or vegetable oil.

3. Mix the flour, water, salt, and vegetable oil into a stiff dough.

4. Spread the dough out flat on the greased cookie sheet.

5. Bake for 30 minutes.

6. Remove from the oven and cut the dough into 3-inch squares. Use a fork to prick holes in the dough.

7. Bake for another 30 minutes.

8. Let the hardtack cook completely before eating.

INGREDIENTS AND SUPPLIES

- cookie sheet
- 3 cups flour
- 1 cup water
- 1 teaspoon salt
- 1 tablespoon vegetable oil

Craft: Make a Flipbook

In the 1800s there were no movies or television. There was a machine called a zoetrope that created what seemed to be moving pictures. The zoetrope was invented in 1834. It was a metal drum with an open top and slits on the side. Inside the drum was a ring of paper with images on it. Viewers looked through the slit as the drum was spinning. The images seemed to move. You can create a similar experience by making a flipbook.

A zoetrope shows images similar to a flipbook.

Make sure to read all the directions before starting the project.

SUPPLIES

- **3** sheets of letter-sized blank paper
- pencils or markers
- stapler

1. Cut each sheet of paper in half, lengthwise. Put all 6 strips of paper in a stack and straighten. Fold the whole pile in half like a book. Staple the fold so that your book stays together. (See picture A)

2. Choose a movement to illustrate. Some examples: a man walking, a horse running, a flower growing. *What movement might children in the 1800s choose?*

3. Think about the steps in the movement. For example, the drawings in picture B show the first three movements of a man walking.

4. Draw your movement one step at a time, in order. Try to place your drawing in the same spot on each piece of paper. You may wish to practice the drawings on a blank piece of paper first. Color your drawings if you'd like.

Hold the flipbook in one hand. Use the other hand to quickly flip through the pages. Watch the movement!

Activity: Create a Secret Code

Spies and secret codes have always been a part of war. A spy pretends to support one side in a conflict but is really working for the other side. Rose O'Neil Greenhow was a Civil War spy. She lived in Washington, D.C., which was part of the Union, but she supported the Confederacy. She sent information about the Union army to leaders of the Confederate army. Her messages were often in code.

Rose O'Neal Greenhow was a spy for the Confederacy. This photograph with her daughter was taken in a prison in Washington, D.C.

One kind of code used during the Civil War was called a transposition code. Letters or words were scrambled so the message didn't make sense. However, anyone who knew how the message had been scrambled could read it.

This message is written in a transposition code.

TOPAEACIGOT/ROSRMRHNSUH

You can read the message if you know the secret. The slash mark breaks the message into two parts. Write out the first set of letters, leaving a space after each letter. Write the second set underneath, below the spaces.

T		O		P		A		E		A		C		I		G		O		T	
	R		O		S		R		M		R		H		N		S		U		H

To read the message, rewrite it starting at the top left with the T. Then go to the second line (R). Go to the top (O), then to the bottom (O). Keep going from top to bottom as you move from left to right, until you run out of letters.

TROOPSAREMARCHINGSOUTH

Now look for the words in the message. If you found the message "TROOPS ARE MARCHING SOUTH," you broke the code! Now you are ready to try writing your own secret message using a transposition code.

In addition to traditional spies and secret messages, other forms of spying were used during the Civil War. Women often dressed as men and passed messages to their side. Notes were hidden in jewlery or clothing of both men and women. Both the Union and Confederate armies used hot air balloons to spy on the other side. This was the first time in U.S. history that balloons were used for this purpose. The first Union balloon was launched in 1861 near Arlington, Virginia. It allowed Union troops to accurately shoot at Confederate troops without being seen.

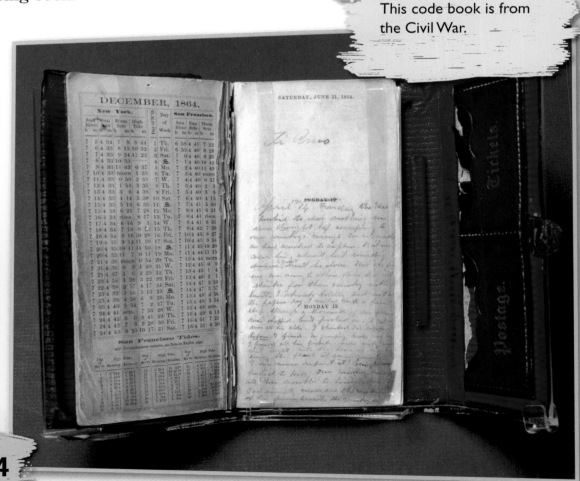

This code book is from the Civil War.

Write in Code

1. Work with your partner to come up with a plan for scrambling letters or words. For example, you could use a zigzag plan like the code on the previous page, but you could write the words backward. Or you could have certain letters of the alphabet stand for other letters. *Is it possible to create a code using something other than letters?*

2. Once you decide on a plan, write messages to each other.

3. Use the plan to break the code and read the message.

4. You can test your code by sending a message to someone who doesn't know the plan. That person shouldn't be able to read the message until you tell him or her how.

This ring opened up so that a secret message could be hidden inside it.

Craft: Create a Quilt Pattern

In the 1840s, the textile industry made fabric available to most women in the United States. Quilting became a popular way for women to express their creativity. It was also a way for them to make blankets for their home.

Enslaved women in the South often made quilts. The women would take pieces of material from old clothes and sew them together. Then they would use raw cotton as stuffing. Some women made quilts using shapes and patterns brought over from Africa. Others used scenes from the well-known stories. Some women sewed secret messages into their quilts. These hidden messages were sometimes used to help slaves escape.

This quilt is from the late 19th century.

SUPPLIES

- needle
- thread
- nylon stockings or other stuffing material (available at craft stores)
- four six-inch squares of cotton fabric (can be old or new)
- fabric-safe markers

A

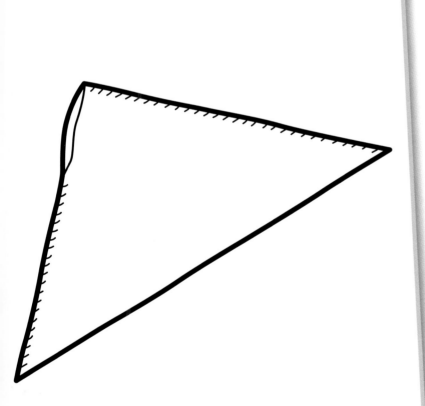

1. Fold one square of material over as a triangle, wrong side out.

2. Sew both sides, leaving a small opening. (See picture A)

3. Turn the triangle right side out.

4. Gently stuff one pair of nylon stockings into the opening. (See picture B)

5. Repeat steps 1–4 for the rest of the triangles.

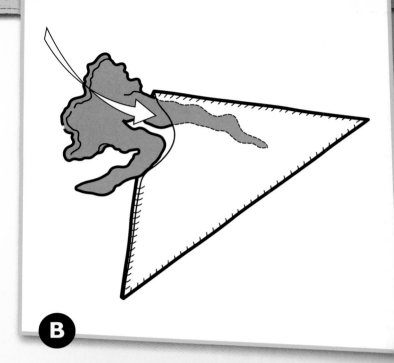

B

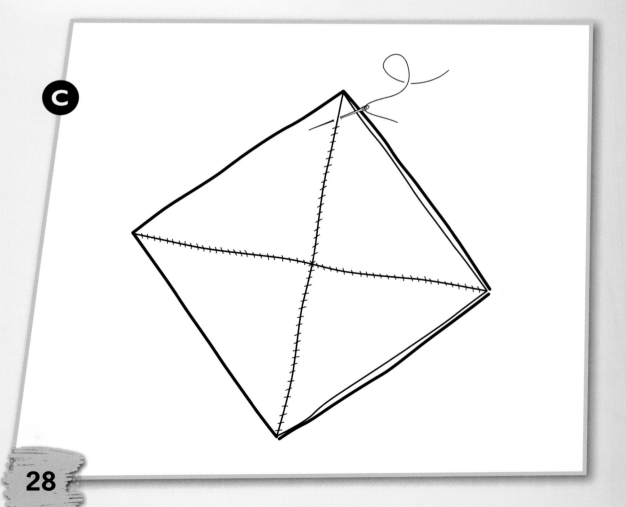

C

6. Sew the triangles together, forming a square. (See picture C.)

7. If you wish, use your markers to create a pattern on the quilt before or after making the triangles. *How many images would you need to draw to tell a story or send a message?*

Glossary

abolitionist person who is against slavery

blockade blocking of a port so ships cannot enter or leave

colonial relating to colonies. A colony is an area ruled by another country.

plantation large estate with many workers

secede to withdraw from or leave

siege placing of an army around a place in order to capture it

territory area that belongs to a country but is not a full part of the country

More Books to Read

Damon, Duane. *Growing Up in the Civil War*. Minneapolis: Lerner, 2003.

Smolinski, Diane. *The Home Front in the North*. Chicago: Heinemann, 2002.

Smolinski, Diane. *The Home Front in the South*. Chicago: Heinemann, 2002.

A Note to Teachers

The instructions for these projects are designed to allow students to work as independently as possible. However, it is always a good idea to make a prototype before assigning any project, so that students can see how their own work will look when completed. Prior to introducing these projects, teachers should collect and prepare the materials and be ready for any modifications that may be necessary. Participating in the project-making process will help teachers understand the directions and be ready to assist students with difficult steps. Teachers might also choose to adapt or modify the lessons to better suit the needs of an individual student or class. No one knows what levels of achievement students will reach better than their teacher.

While it is preferable for students to work as independently as possible, there is some flexibility in regards to project materials and tools. They can vary according to what is available. For instance, while standard white glue may be most familiar to students, there might be times when a teacher will choose to simplify a project by using a hot glue gun to fasten materials for students. Likewise, while a project may call for leather cord, it is feasible in most instances to substitute vinyl cord or even yarn or rope. In another instance, acrylic paint may be recommended because it adheres better to a material like felt or plastic, but other types of paint would be useable as well. The materials and tools that one uses can vary according to what is available. For example, circles can be drawn with a compass, or simply by tracing a cup, roll of tape, or other circular object. Obviously, allowing students a broad spectrum of creativity and opportunities to problem-solve within the parameters of a given project will encourage their critical thinking skills most fully.

Each project contains an italicized question somewhere in the directions. These questions are meant to be thought-provoking and promote discussion while students work on the project.

31

Index